How to use this workbook

Structure

The activities in this workbook help you develop the skills and knowledge that y...
grade in A-level English Literature, whichever exam board specification you are f...

Each section offers a clear structure with activities that gradually increase in difficulty:

- **Starting out:** accessible activities that offer an introduction to the topic
- **Developing your ideas:** skills-building activities that look in more detail at particular aspects of the text
- **Taking it further:** more challenging tasks that will test your understanding of the text and consolidate your learning

Boosting your skills

The final chapter of the workbook offers exam-focused activities that allow you to apply the skills you have developed. It also includes step-by-step guidance on the Assessment Objectives, and how to cover them in your written responses.

Features

Key terms

Definitions of key concepts and terminology. Understanding these and using them correctly in your written responses will help gain marks for AO1.

Key skills

Concise explanations of important skills to develop during your A-level studies. A variety of skills are covered, from fundamental ones such as analysing the structure of a text or embedding quotations in your writing, up to more advanced skills that are necessary to gain the top grades, such as exploring different interpretations of characters.

Challenge yourself

Advanced tasks that will push you further and help prepare you to achieve your best grade in the exams. They often focus on context (AO3), connections between texts (AO4) or critical interpretations of them (AO5).

Introduction: studying *Othello* at A-level

Your Shakespeare study for Key Stage 3 and GCSE will form a good basis for A-level. However, you will now have to extend your existing skills. In particular, you will need to be more aware of the possible critical approaches to the play, which is why this workbook devotes a chapter to them. You will also need to consider the play's social, historical and cultural context, and so one chapter in this workbook focuses on that. At the very least, you should be able to compare *Othello* with another Shakespeare play that you have studied, which will help to throw *Othello* into perspective. Obviously, knowing other tragedies like *Macbeth* or *Romeo and Juliet* will be helpful, but *Othello* also has a surprising amount in common with some of Shakespeare's comedies, especially *Much Ado About Nothing*.

Above all, you need to develop your own interpretation of the play and be able to express this fluently, backing up your arguments with evidence from the text. You will be more fluent if you master the art of using short embedded quotations within your own sentences.

Characters

The study of characters remains important at A-level, but you will be expected to have a deeper awareness of their dramatic roles and the dynamics between them. You should avoid falling into the trap of writing about them as if they are real people. One interpretation of Iago, for example, is that he is not supposed to be psychologically realistic; instead, he is a traditional villain, like the devil in medieval mystery plays. According to this view, there is little point in trying to work out his motives for villainy.

Themes and language

Themes remain important, but you will need to show more awareness of how they are reflected in the language of the play, and be able to demonstrate how Shakespeare's language achieves its effects. In doing this, you will need to make correct use of technical terms such as 'metaphor' and 'simile'.

Gaining an overview

You will probably read the play in class, but it will help if you read it to yourself as well. When you have read the text and understood the plot and the character relationships, you need to develop an overview of the play. Ideally, you should be able to remember which Act any major event or speech occurs in, and perhaps even which scene, so that you can find it easily. This will help you when looking for quotes or comparing scenes. The 'Plot and structure' section in this workbook will help you to achieve this. An overview will also enable you to analyse the play's narrative arc and to relate this to the genre of tragedy.

Using the workbook

You do not necessarily have to attempt all the activities in the workbook: you could pick and choose according to your needs. However, there is a progression within each section, from the basics in 'Starting out' to 'Taking it further'. In addition, 'Challenge yourself' boxes aim to push you that little bit further to help you achieve the top grades. You should also take note of the 'Key skills' and 'Key terms' boxes.

Line references are to the Arden Shakespeare edition. They are given in short form: so, 1.2.3 refers to Act 1, scene 2, line 3. This will vary slightly in other editions, but the short quotations will help you to overcome this variation.

Plot and structure

A sound knowledge of *Othello*'s plot is essential in the exam. Ideally you will also know in which Acts the key events occur. This will help you to write about the play's structure.

STARTING OUT

1 Shakespeare based *Othello* on a story by an Italian author, Cinthio. We can assume that any plot changes are significant to his dramatic purpose or made the story easier to stage.
Read this summary of Cinthio's story. Look for differences between it and the plot of *Othello*.

> A virtuous young Venetian woman, Disdemona, falls in love with a brave Moor and marries him against her family's wishes. They live happily in Venice for some time until the Moor is appointed Commander of Cyprus. Disdemona wants to stay with him, so they sail together. The Moor has a 'scoundrelly' Ensign with an honest young wife and a three-year-old daughter. The Ensign falls in love with Disdemona. She ignores him, so he assumes she must love a Corporal who visits her home. The Ensign seeks revenge by accusing the pair of adultery. Soon after, the Moor dismisses the Corporal for wounding another soldier.
>
> Disdemona tries to persuade the Moor to reinstate the Corporal. The Ensign hints to the Moor that she has good reason, but refuses to say more, which torments the Moor, who threatens Disdemona. The Ensign now claims that Disdemona and the Corporal are lovers. The Moor demands proof, so the Ensign visits Disdemona, and while handing his child to Disdemona steals her handkerchief, which he leaves in the Corporal's room. He then arranges for the Moor to overhear him with the laughing Corporal. The Ensign claims that the Corporal has confessed and that Disdemona gave him the handkerchief.
>
> One day the Moor asks Disdemona for the handkerchief. She pretends to look for it, but of course cannot find it. The Moor now considers killing her. She sees he has changed towards her and asks for the advice of the Ensign's wife, who is too afraid to reveal the Ensign's plot. The Corporal asks a woman who works for him to copy the embroidery of the handkerchief. The Moor sees her doing this, and asks the Ensign to kill the Corporal. The Ensign slices through the Corporal's leg while he is leaving a courtesan's house.
>
> The Ensign and Moor bludgeon Disdemona with a sandbag and make it look as if she has died in a ceiling collapse. The Moor misses her, and blames the Ensign, so the Ensign tells the Corporal (who now has a wooden leg) that it was the Moor who cut his leg off and killed Disdemona. The Moor is arrested, tortured and exiled, and then murdered by Disdemona's family. The Ensign is imprisoned and tortured for another crime, dying of his wounds.

CONTINUED →

In the table below, add what you think are the five most important changes (apart from names), and Shakespeare's possible reasons for making them.

CHANGE IN THE PLAY	POSSIBLE REASON(S)
1	
2	
3	
4	
5	

2   In which Act does each of these events occur?

EVENT		ACT
A	Desdemona and Emilia discuss adultery	
B	Othello marries Desdemona	
C	Emilia gives Iago the handkerchief	
D	Othello kills Desdemona	
E	Cassio gets into a drunken brawl and is dismissed	

KEY SKILLS

Commenting on plot

You will earn little credit by simply retelling the story of the play. Examiners regard this as an indicator of a weak candidate. However, you could comment on how and why Shakespeare's plot differs from that of his main source.

DEVELOPING YOUR IDEAS

3 Once you are sure of the plot, you need to consider the structure. One widely accepted theory is that most stories follow a five-point design. Make notes below on how this could apply to *Othello*.

Point 1: The initiating incident that triggers the main action. What is this in *Othello*? When does it happen? How does it trigger further action? Is there any doubt about what the incident is?

....

....

....

....

Point 2: Successes and reverses for the protagonist – Othello. How is he successful? At what point do things start to go wrong? Is there a key point when he seems doomed? What are the stages in his descent?

....

....

....

....

Point 3: Crisis, when there is most at stake for the protagonist. Is there just one crisis, when in theory Othello could still step back from disaster?

....

....

....

....

Point 4: Climax – the most dramatically intense moment of the play. What is this, and what makes it intense? Is there a moment of final suspense involved?

....

....

....

....

Point 5: Resolution – in a tragedy, the restoration of social order and emotional equilibrium, when the audience should feel catharsis. How secure does Cyprus seem after Othello's death? Is it in safe hands, with a secure future? Has justice been done?

....

....

....

....

CONTINUED ➔

Initiating incident: event that can be said to trigger all the subsequent action of a play.

Catharsis: Ancient Greek term for the sense of emotional calm that the audience should feel at the end of a tragedy, as if emotions have been purged and balance has been restored.

4   For there to be a true resolution and catharsis in a tragedy, the hero must achieve self-understanding, and accept the mistakes he has made. How far do you feel this is the case with Othello? Comment on his attitude to:

●   Desdemona

....

....

....

●   Himself

....

....

....

●   Iago

....

....

....

●   Cassio

....

....

....

....

5   An important element of the plot that would be more evident on stage than in your reading of the play is setting. Shakespeare uses setting, including time of day, to create atmospheres that are appropriate to the action, and to vary the mood of the play.

Use the table on the next page to record the settings, the main action that occurs in each, and how each setting creates an atmosphere that fits the action and contributes to the overall development of the play. The first has been done for you.

CONTINUED ➡

SCENE	WHERE AND WHEN	MAIN ACTION	HOW IT FITS
1.1	Street in Venice, night	Iago and Roderigo tell Brabantio that Desdemona has married Othello.	Night creates uncertainty. Street is public, creating possible shame.
1.2			
1.3			
2.1			
2.2			
2.3			
3.1			
3.2			
3.3			
3.4			
4.1			
4.2			
4.3			
5.1			
5.2			
SCENE	WHERE AND WHEN	MAIN ACTION	HOW IT FITS
		Iago and Roderigo tell Brabantio that	Night creates uncertainty. Street

TAKING IT FURTHER

6   *Othello* has a 'double time scheme': 'short' and 'long'. Shakespeare's main source, Cinthio's story, operates in 'long time'. For example, Othello and Disdemona live together for some time before travelling to Cyprus. Therefore, Shakespeare must have had a purpose in making it seem that the play's events are spread over several weeks *and* over a much shorter time – 33 hours.

Divide the events and references below into (S)hort or (L)ong time.

EVENT OR REFERENCE		SHORT (S) OR LONG (L)
A	Othello is sent urgently to Cyprus immediately after his marriage has been discovered.	
B	Othello and Desdemona voyage to Cyprus by sea. Meanwhile the Turkish fleet heads towards Rhodes and is wrecked.	
C	Othello and Desdemona arrive in Cyprus on Saturday afternoon. (2.2)	
D	Cassio gets drunk and is dismissed on Saturday night. (2.3.13)	
E	Cassio decides to ask Desdemona to help him 'betimes in the morning'. (2.3.324)	
F	Iago persuades Othello completely of Desdemona's infidelity in the space of one scene. (3.3)	
G	Emilia: 'My wayward husband hath a hundred times/ Wooed me to steal it.' (3.3.296–7)	
H	Bianca: 'What, keep a week away?' (3.4.173)	
I	Bianca: 'What did you mean by that handkerchief you gave me even now?' (4.1.147–9)	
J	Othello: '… she with Cassio hath the act of shame/ A thousand times committed.' (5.2.209–10)	

7   What do you think Shakespeare achieves dramatically, and in terms of credibility, by introducing 'short time'? How well do you think this works on stage?

....

....

....

....

....

....

....

KEY SKILLS

Seeing the audience's perspective

Always bear in mind how the play would seem to a live audience. Although Shakespeare's 'short' and 'long' time schemes contradict each other, this would not be obvious to any but the most observant audience members.

8 Shakespeare has varied the pace of the play quite noticeably at times. In particular, there is one very quiet scene, Act 4, scene 3, in which it could be said that nothing happens, at least after Othello tells Desdemona to go to bed. After this, Desdemona prepares for bed and talks with Emilia.

Imagine you are directing the play. Your producer wants to cut this scene completely to reduce the play's running time. Write a memo arguing for keeping it on the basis of it being dramatically necessary at this point in the play.

....

....

....

....

....

....

....

....

....

9 *Much Ado About Nothing*, Act 3, scene 4, is similar to Act 4, scene 3 of *Othello*. It features women talking privately while one of them, Hero, dresses for her wedding. She does not know it, but she is about to be cruelly jilted at the altar.

Find this play online or in book form, read the scene, and write a paragraph comparing it with the scene in *Othello*. Focus especially on dramatic purpose.

....

....

....

....

....

....

....

....

....

Challenge yourself

The 'short time' scheme makes it possible that Othello and Desdemona have not had time to consummate their marriage. What do you think the uncertainty over this achieves dramatically? Bear in mind the context of Jacobean values.

Themes

Themes usually relate to universal human concerns, such as love. However, some themes are more contextual. Several Shakespeare plays explore the theme of kingship, which is unlikely to feature in a modern novel; but Shakespeare never explores the theme of science, because it was not yet an issue in his era.

STARTING OUT

1   There is no definitive list of themes in *Othello*, but critics generally agree on four or five being especially important. From the typical Shakespearean themes below, circle the four that you think feature most in *Othello*.

Kingship	Love and sex	Money and wealth	Fate	The supernatural
Jealousy	Revenge	Death	Ambition	Parent–child relationships
Appearance and reality	Nobility	Prejudice	Forgiveness	Individuals and society
Envy	Greed	Honour		

2   For each theme that you circled, explain how it contributes to the play's tragic outcome.

(a) ....

....

(b) ....

....

(c) ....

....

(d) ....

....

3   Comment on how each of the quotations below relates to one or more themes. Hint: Notice the language used – for example, **personification**.

(a) Othello: I cannot speak enough of this content,/ It stops me here, it is too much of joy.

....

....

(b) Emilia: It is a monster/ Begot upon itself, born on itself.

....

....

(c) Iago: Faith, he tonight hath boarded a land carrack.

....

....

CONTINUED ➔

Answers can be found at: www.hoddereducation.co.uk/workbookanswers

(d) Brabantio: Damned as thou art, thou hast enchanted her,

....

....

(e) Iago: Men should be what they seem,/ Or those that be not, would they might seem none.

....

....

(f) Cassio: Reputation, reputation, reputation! O, I have lost my reputation,

....

....

Personification: an image in which something – especially something abstract like jealousy – is spoken of as if it is a conscious being.

DEVELOPING YOUR IDEAS

4   **Love and sex**

Which characters show the following attitudes towards love and sex? Add at least one short quotation or reference to support your choice.

(a) Love is really just lust – an expression of our base animal nature.

   Character: .... Evidence: ....

   ....

   ....

(b) True love can grow from mutual admiration and appreciation – a reciprocal relationship in which each fulfils the other.

   Character: .... Evidence: ....

   ....

   ....

(c) Some women should be respected, almost worshipped, while others may be treated as sexual playthings.

   Character: .... Evidence: ....

   ....

   ....

(d) A woman should show her love by being meek and obedient to her husband, however he behaves.

   Character: .... Evidence: ....

   ....

   ....

CONTINUED →

(e) Women are exploited and abused by men, and should stand up to them.

Character: .... Evidence: ....

....

5   Which of the attitudes above do you think would be seen most differently by Jacobean and modern audiences? Explain your choice.

....

....

....

....

6   Jealousy

(a) Complete the table below to show the view of jealousy that Shakespeare presents in each of these quotations, and how imagery contributes to this.

QUOTATION	VIEW	IMAGERY
Iago: O beware, my lord, of jealousy! It is the green–eyed monster which doth mock The meat it feeds on.	*Jealousy is a dangerous emotion …*	
Othello: I had been happy, if the general camp, Pioneers and all, had tasted her sweet body, So I had nothing known.		*The metaphor of soldiers 'tasting' Desdemona …*
Desdemona: … and but my noble Moor Is true of mind, and made of no such baseness As jealous creatures are, it were enough To put him to ill–thinking.	*Desdemona sees jealousy as …*	

CONTINUED

(b) 'Jealousy makes Othello too pathetic a figure to be called a tragic hero.' Bearing in mind the table above, how far do you agree with this statement? Explain your opinion.

....

....

....

....

....

7   Reread the key scene in the development of Othello's jealousy: Act 3, scene 3, from 'Give me a living reason she's disloyal.' (line 412) to the end of the scene. Then answer these questions:

(a) What do you think is the significance of Othello's 'Give me a living reason she's disloyal'?

....

....

(b) Explain how Iago begins his 'living reason' in order to increase his plausibility.

....

....

....

(c) What do you find interesting about Iago choosing to provide 'proof' in the form of the dream, and how convincing Othello finds it?

....

....

....

....

(d) How does Iago make his next 'proof', involving the handkerchief, more effective?

....

....

....

(e) How do you imagine Othello might continue his line 'If it be that –' (line 442) if he were to complete it?

....

....

CONTINUED ➡

(f) Read this opening to an analysis of how Othello's jealousy develops in this scene. Then, on a separate sheet, write at least one more paragraph continuing on from it, to cover the text as far as Othello's 'If it be that –'.

At this point in the scene, Iago has been working Othello to a fever pitch of jealous doubt, but Othello has not yet given in entirely. He still requires proof, a 'living reason she's disloyal', before he will accept Desdemona's infidelity as a fact. Iago realises that Othello is now jealous enough to believe an unsubstantiated account of a dream as 'proof', and that Othello now almost wants to hear this 'proof' rather than remain in the agony of uncertainty.

8 How far do you think this passage, from line 412 to the end of the scene, shows that Othello is naturally jealous?

....

....

....

9 **Appearance and reality**

(a) Many things in *Othello* are not what they seem, and uncertainty pervades the play, including Othello's initial uncertainty about Desdemona's fidelity. Give each of the factors below a score of 1–3 according to how you see its persuasive strength as evidence of Desdemona's guilt.

EVIDENCE	SCORE
She deceived her father to marry Othello.	
Cassio apparently sneaking away from Desdemona	
Her efforts to have Cassio reinstated	
Iago says Cassio wiped his beard with Desdemona's handkerchief	
Iago's account of Cassio talking in his sleep	
Othello observes Cassio laughing with Iago	
Venetian women, says Iago, have loose morals	

(b) Which statement do you think is more true? Give your reasons.
  (i) Othello is naturally jealous and a gullible fool.
  (ii) It is reasonable for Othello to think Desdemona guilty on the evidence provided.

....

....

....

....

CONTINUED ➡

10 Race and prejudice

(a) Fill in the blanks with suitable words from the list underneath to complete this paragraph on the theme of prejudice in the play.

Although .... England was far from ...., there were enough black

people in London for Elizabeth I to have wanted them to be .... Hence there

would be some understanding of Othello's position as a Moorish ....

He is respected as a ...., and he .... that Brabantio 'loved'

and 'oft invited' him, but this does not .... to wanting him for a

.... Brabantio claims that Othello's marriage to Desdemona is 'Against

all rules of nature', and he .... Othello by accusing him of .... –

'practices of cunning hell'. Roderigo similarly reflects popular .... in referring to

him as a 'lascivious Moor'. Even .... Emilia calls him Desdemona's 'filthy bargain'.

asserts	deported	extend	fair-minded	Georgian	infidelity	intolerant
Jacobean	jokes	king	lead	lovely	multicultural	murdered
outsider	prejudices	pretends	sailor	soldier	son-in-law	stereotypes
upsets	villain	witchcraft				

(b) Reread Act 3, scene 3, lines 261–81:

> This fellow's of exceeding honesty
> And knows all qualities, with a learned spirit,
> Of human dealings. If I do prove her haggard,
> Though that her jesses were my dear heart-strings,
> I'd whistle her off and let her down the wind
> To prey at fortune. Haply for I am black
> And have not those soft parts of conversation
> That chamberers have, or for I am declined
> Into the vale of years - yet that's not much -
> She's gone, I am abused, and my relief
> Must be to loathe her. O curse of marriage
> That we can call these delicate creatures ours
> And not their appetites! I had rather be a toad
> And live upon the vapour of a dungeon
> Than keep a corner in the thing I love
> For others' uses. Yet, 'tis the plague of great ones,
> Prerogatived are they less than the base;

CONTINUED ➡

'Tis destiny unshunnable, like death -

Even then this forked plague is fated to us

When we do quicken.

Now consider this statement:

'The root of Othello's jealous suspicions is the prejudice he experiences as an outsider in Venetian society.'

Annotate the quotation to show lines that might support or challenge this statement, and then write a paragraph explaining how far you agree. Consider both this passage and the play as a whole.

Challenge yourself

How important do you think it is nowadays for Othello to be played by a black actor? Consider this question in relation to what differences you think there would be between a Shakespearean audience's perception of the play and that of a modern audience.

11 Individuals and society

People in Shakespeare's Venice, as in Jacobean England, want to be socially accepted.

(a) Find evidence in the form of references or short quotations to support the numbered statements in the paragraph below.

Iago feels rejected when Othello promotes Cassio instead of him.[1] Then, thanks to Iago exploiting his weakness for alcohol, Cassio is convinced that now he will be rejected.[2]

Othello, perhaps naively, felt accepted by Brabantio.[3] However, when he becomes jealous, he starts to wonder if Desdemona is prejudiced against him because of his colour.[4]

1 ....

....

2 ....

....

3 ....

....

4 ....

....

CONTINUED ➡

(b) Rewrite the four sentences using your evidence. Add analysis of your evidence. Use at least some embedded quotations, and vary the order in which the Point, Evidence and Analysis are presented.

....

....

....

....

....

....

....

....

....

....

....

KEY SKILLS

Embedding quotations

It is often effective to embed quotations, making them part of your sentence. When you do this, you should select what you quote so that your sentence works grammatically. For example: 'Brabantio regards racially mixed marriage as being "Against all rules of nature".'

TAKING IT FURTHER

12 Now that you have worked on all the separate themes, this activity should help you see how they connect. In the table below, explain how each of the quotations relates to at least two themes.

QUOTATION	YOUR EXPLANATION
A Duke of Venice Whoe'er he be, that in this foul proceeding Hath thus beguiled your daughter of herself, And you of her, the bloody book of law You shall yourself read, in the bitter letter, (1.3.66–9)	
B Iago Reputation is an idle and most false imposition, oft got without merit and lost without deserving. You have lost no reputation at all, unless you repute yourself such a loser. (2.3.264–7)	
C Othello Haply for I am black And have not those soft parts of conversation That chamberers have, or for I am declined Into the vale of years – yet that's not much – She's gone, I am abused, (3.3.267–71)	
D Iago In sleep I heard him say 'Sweet Desdemona, Let us be wary, let us hide our loves,' (3.3.421–2)	
E Desdemona Who, he? I think the sun where he was born Drew all such humours from him. (3.4.30–1)	

CONTINUED ➜

Answers can be found at: www.hoddereducation.co.uk/workbookanswers

13 Consider which of the following possible additional themes for *Othello* you think could be the most important. Circle your top two.

Social class   Loyalty   Reputation   War   Law   Uncertainty   Nature of humanity

On a separate sheet, write a paragraph explaining how each of your top two additional themes features in the play. Add a final short paragraph explaining which of the two you think is more important.

14 Reread Act 2, scene 1, lines 180–211 (from 'Othello: O my fair warrior' to 'Once more, well met at Cyprus').

(a) Write one or more paragraphs exploring how Shakespeare presents love in this passage. Consider:

- what Othello and Desdemona say and do
- what language is used – for example, imagery
- hints of what is to come later in the play.

(b) Write at least one more paragraph on how other aspects of love are presented in the play.

CONTINUED

(c) Write a paragraph arguing either for or against the view that *Othello* is primarily a play about hatred rather than about love.

....

....

....

....

....

....

....

Challenge yourself

'Love and sex are the opposite poles of the play, not coming together, disturbingly unassimilated to one another' (John Bayley, 'Tragedy and Consciousness: *Othello*'). Find evidence for this view in Shakespeare's portrayal of Othello, Desdemona and Iago.

Characterisation

Character overview

To get to grips with the characters in *Othello*, you need to think about their motivation, and how they relate to each other. You also need to be able to discuss different interpretations. For example, is Iago really seeking revenge, or is he just malicious?

STARTING OUT

1   Shakespeare often includes parallels between characters. Find *two* characters to match each of the descriptions below.

DESCRIPTION	CHARACTERS
A Tricked by Iago	
B Regard Desdemona as beautiful	
C Mistreated by their spouses	
D Resent their treatment by Othello	
E Not valued by their partner	
F Enjoyed Othello's stories	
G Tell Othello that Desdemona may prove unfaithful	

DEVELOPING YOUR IDEAS

2   Complete the statements below to indicate the speaker and what the line reveals.

(a) When .... says 'Ha, I like not that' it is not obvious what he is referring to. This technique

....

....

(b) .... 's comment, 'What a full fortune does the thicklips owe' shows both his

....

(c) ....'s instruction, 'Keep up your bright swords, for the dew will rust them,' shows that at

this point early in the play he is ....

....

CONTINUED ➤

(d) Although often seen as passive, ... shows in the line 'I have not deserved this' that

....

....

(e) ....'s .... attitude towards men is shown by her comment that 'They are all

but stomachs, and we all but food'.

(f) .... feels .... :

he says, 'I have lost the immortal part of myself – and what remains is bestial.'

(g) The .... of ....'s mood now is shown by his vow to 'chop her into messes'.

KEY SKILLS

Inferring

Be aware of what could be implied by the exact words Shakespeare gives to a character. For example, in the exercise above, 'thicklips' implies something about the speaker's attitude. It is not just a neutral physical description.

TAKING IT FURTHER

3   Write one or more paragraphs giving your views on this statement:
    'All the main characters in *Othello* are equally flawed.'

....

....

....

....

....

....

....

....

Answers can be found at: www.hoddereducation.co.uk/workbookanswers

Othello

STARTING OUT

1 Circle the three words below that you think most apply to Othello:

proud   foolish   deluded   warrior   dishonest   brave   arrogant   murderous

2 In the boxes below, write statements that might be made about Othello by each of these characters at different times.

Brabantio

Start of play
....
....
....

After marriage is discovered
....
....
....

Iago

Start of play
....
....
....

End of play
....
....
....

Desdemona

Start of play
....
....
....

After Othello hits her
....
....
....

DEVELOPING YOUR IDEAS

3 Read this speech in Act 1, scene 2 and annotate it to show what key personality traits the underlined lines indicate in Othello.

Let him do his spite;

My services, which I have done the signiory,

Shall out-tongue his complaints.[1] 'Tis yet to know–

Which, when I know that boasting is an honour,

I shall promulgate – I fetch my life and being

From men of royal siege, and my demerits

May speak unbonneted to as proud a fortune

As this that I have reached.[2] For know, Iago,

But that I love the gentle Desdemona

I would not my unhoused free condition

Put into circumscription and confine

For the sea's worth.[3]

CONTINUED ⮕

4 How does this speech, Othello's first of any length, introduce him as a worthy tragic hero?

....

....

....

....

5 Number these lines in order, to show how Othello's jealousy develops as the play progresses. Add a note on how each line shows this development. Start by working out the first and last lines.

LINES	ORDER 1–10	HOW IT SHOWS DEVELOPMENT
A All my fond love thus do I blow to heaven:/ 'Tis gone!		
B Damn her, lewd minx: O damn her, damn her!		
C I swear 'tis better to be much abused/ Than but to know't a little.		
D I took you for that cunning whore of Venice/ That married with Othello. You! Mistress!		
E No, Iago,/ I'll see before I doubt, when I doubt, prove		
F Noses, ears, and lips. Is't possible? Confess! handkerchief! O devil!		
G Put out the light, and then put out the light!		
H She's gone, I am abused, and my relief/ Must be to loathe her.		
I Villain, be sure thou prove my love a whore,/ Be sure of it, give me the ocular proof.		
J Within these three days let me hear thee say/ That Cassio's not alive.		

CONTINUED ➡

6 Referring to **Activity 5**, give your views on how Othello changes during the course of the play and how this relates to the genre of tragedy. Use short quotations from selected lines to back up your analysis.

....

....

....

....

....

....

....

....

TAKING IT FURTHER

7 Read the two views of Othello below.

Which critic's view do you agree with more? On a separate sheet, make notes, a spidergram or a concept map showing your views. Back them up with references to the text.

AC Bradley

A noble victim, 'indisposed to jealousy', yet 'unusually open to deception, and, if once wrought to passion, likely to act with little reflection'.

(*Shakespearean Tragedy*, 1904)

FR Leavis

Othello causes his own downfall by being egotistical, narcissistic (self-loving), self-dramatising, and credulous.

('Diabolic Intellect and the Noble Hero', 1952)

Challenge yourself

Bearing in mind the views of Bradley and Leavis, and your knowledge of other Shakespearean tragedies, how do you rate Othello as a tragic hero? At the end of the play, do you regard him as a truly noble man destroyed by evil, or as something less than this?

Iago

STARTING OUT

1   Critics have long debated why Iago chooses to ruin Othello. But there are some things we definitely know about Iago. Which statements below are definitely true?

(a) He thinks he should have been promoted instead of Cassio. True/False

(b) He has an idealised and romantic view of love. True/False

(c) He admires Cassio's mathematical ability. True/False

(d) He is not a noble. True/False

(e) He is materialistic, repeatedly telling Roderigo to acquire as much money as he can. True/False

(f) He claims to suspect both Othello and Cassio of having had sex with Emilia. True/False

(g) He is a good friend to Roderigo. True/False

(h) He is secretly homosexual. True/False

2   Now summarise the true statements as a paragraph describing Iago in your own words.

....

....

....

....

....

....

....

DEVELOPING YOUR IDEAS

3   What in your view does each of Iago's lines below show about him?

LINE	WHAT IT SHOWS
I know my price, I am worth no worse a place.	
Even now, now, very now, an old black ram/ Is tupping your white ewe!	
For I do know the state,/ However this may gall him with some check,/ Cannot with safety cast him.	
Though in the trade of war I have slain men/ Yet do I hold it very stuff o'th' conscience/ To do no contrived murder	
Faith, he tonight hath boarded a land carrack	
Men should be what they seem,/ Or those that be not, would they might seem none.	
Demand me nothing. What you know, you know./ From this time forth I never will speak word.	

CONTINUED ➡

4   On a separate sheet, write one or more paragraphs analysing Iago's relationships with other characters in the play. Back up what you say with evidence in the form of references or short quotations.

TAKING IT FURTHER

5   (a) Summarise what belief Iago expresses in this speech to Roderigo:

'Virtue? A fig! 'tis in ourselves that we are thus, or thus. Our bodies are gardens, to the which our wills are gardeners.' (1.3.320–2)

....

....

....

....

....

(b) Iago is a villain. He could be compared with another resentful villain, Edmund, in Shakespeare's tragedy *King Lear*. Edmund dismisses the idea that character is shaped by astrology:

My father compounded with my mother under the dragon's tail; and my nativity was under Ursa Major; so that it follows, I am rough and lecherous. Tut, I should have been that I am, had the maidenliest star in the firmament twinkled on my bastardising.

Compare the views and characters of Iago and Edmund as shown in these two speeches.

....

....

....

....

....

....

Villain: a stock figure (possibly arising from portrayals of Satan in medieval religious plays) who is not a fully rounded character, and who may play a large part in the hero's downfall.

Tragedy: a play in the tragic genre, in which the downfall and death of an essentially noble hero are brought about by a flaw in their character.

KEY SKILLS

Referring to genre

Although you may not be able to refer in detail to other Shakespeare plays, you should understand the features of *Othello* that make it a tragedy, and how its tragic hero Othello's tragic flaw, arguably, is being credulous (too trusting).

---

6   In Shakespeare's soliloquies, characters always speak the truth – or what they take to be the truth, so that we have an insight into their minds.

Read Iago's soliloquy at the end of Act 1, scene 3, then answer these questions.

(a) What reason does Iago give for hating Othello? How far do you think this reflects his real motives for ruining Othello?

....

....

....

....

(b) What is the dramatic effect of Iago saying 'Let me see now ... How? How? Let's see ... I have't, it is engendered!'

....

....

(c) What could be implied by Iago calling his plan 'this monstrous birth'?

....

....

(d) On a separate sheet, write one or more paragraphs evaluating the dramatic effect of Iago's soliloquies, here and elsewhere in the play.

Soliloquy (plural – soliloquies): a speech spoken by one character alone on stage, either as if thinking aloud or addressing the audience directly.

Challenge yourself

Reread Iago's soliloquy at the end of Act 1, scene 3. Early critic ST Coleridge in 1818 commented that this showed 'the motive-hunting of motiveless malignity', meaning that Iago simply wanted to do evil and was trying to justify this desire. Make two sets of bullet points – one supporting Coleridge's view, and one arguing against it.

Desdemona, Emilia and Bianca

It can be helpful to look at these three female characters together, as well as individually. They all respond in their different ways to the difficulties of being women in a world dominated by men.

STARTING OUT

1 Add ticks to the table below to show what the three women have in common and how they differ. Add question marks where you think there is some uncertainty.

	DESDEMONA	EMILIA	BIANCA
Noble-born			
Commoner			
Admired			
Poor reputation			
Jealous husband			
Unappreciated by men			
Used by men			
Wanting to help or please men			
Falsely accused			
Murdered			

2 Referring to your completed table, write a paragraph about what the women have in common, and how they differ.

....

....

....

....

....

....

....

....

....

....

DEVELOPING YOUR IDEAS

3 Order these adjectives 1–9 according to how far you think they apply to Desdemona.

imaginative	romantic	adventurous	rebellious	naive
....	....	....	....	....

passive	persistent	loyal	virtuous
....	....	....	....

CONTINUED ➡

4 Write a paragraph explaining your reasons for numbering your top three traits above.

....

....

....

....

....

....

5 (a) Read Desdemona's speech beginning 'That I did love the Moor ...' (1.3.249–60). What do you deduce about her character from the lines in the table below?

LINE	WHAT IT SHOWS
My downright violence and scorn of fortunes/ May trumpet to the world.	
Did I my soul and fortunes consecrate	
The rites for which I love him are bereft me	

(b) This is a speech spoken by a teenage girl to the Duke and Senators of Venice. Taken overall, what does it suggest about Desdemona's character?

....

....

....

6 Read the passage from Desdemona's 'O, these men, these men!' to Desdemona's 'I do not think there is any such woman' (4.3.59–82).

(a) What might each woman say about the other's attitudes if they were commenting on this conversation?

....

....

....

....

CONTINUED →

(b) How do you personally evaluate the two women as presented by Shakespeare in this passage?

....

....

....

....

7 **(a)** How does Shakespeare present Bianca, and Cassio's treatment of her, in their conversation at the end of Act 3, beginning 'Save you, friend Cassio!'?

....

....

....

....

(b) How do you personally feel about Bianca when you read this passage?

....

....

....

....

(c) Make notes on how you would direct an actor playing Bianca to perform the role. Explain what impact you would want her to make, bearing in mind how the role might work alongside those of Desdemona and Emilia.

....

....

....

....

TAKING IT FURTHER

8 Read and annotate Emilia's speech in which she addresses Desdemona, seeming to defend unfaithful
wives:

> But I do think it is their husbands' faults
>
> If wives do fall. Say that they slack their duties
>
> And pour our treasures into foreign laps;
>
> Or else break out in peevish jealousies,
>
> Throwing restraint upon us; or say they strike us,
>
> Or scant our former having in despite,
>
> Why, we have galls: and though we have some grace
>
> Yet have we some revenge. Let husbands know
>
> Their wives have sense like them: they see, and smell
>
> And have their palates both for sweet and sour
>
> As husbands have. What is it that they do
>
> When they change us for others? Is it sport?
>
> I think it is. And doth affection breed it?
>
> I think it doth. Is't frailty that thus errs?
>
> It is so too. And have not we affections,
>
> Desires for sport? and frailty, as men have?
>
> Then let them use us well: else let them know,
>
> The ills we do, their ills instruct us so.

(4.3.85–102)

Which of these views of the speech do you most agree with, and why?

(a) Shakespeare is presenting an argument for women's rights and equality.

(b) The speech is intended as a contrast with Desdemona's virtue.

(c) Emilia is simply being realistic, and reacting to her own experience of marriage to Iago.

....

....

CONTINUED ➡

....

....

....

9   Write an essay plan, with notes on what evidence you might use, in answer to the following question:

'In Othello Shakespeare presents women as passive victims, mere pawns in the power-play between the male characters.' How far do you agree, and why?

....

....

....

....

....

....

....

....

....

....

....

....

....

....

....

....

Challenge yourself

One interpretation of the female characters in *Othello* is that they represent the ways in which men objectify and stereotype women. How far do you think this view is justified?

Cassio and Roderigo

STARTING OUT

1   Use this table to help you consider differences and similarities between Cassio and Roderigo. Add ticks where appropriate.

DESCRIPTION	CASSIO	RODERIGO
Admires Desdemona		
Wants to marry Desdemona		
Noble		
Rich		
Courtly manners and speech		
Deceived by Iago		
Gullible		
Gets drunk easily		

2   Circle the words below that you think apply to Cassio or to Roderigo. Use a different colour for each character.

gullible   courtly   stupid   honourable   loyal   moral

DEVELOPING YOUR IDEAS

3   Read what Iago says about Cassio to Roderigo in the opening scene:

> Forsooth, a great arithmetician,
>
> One Michael Cassio, a Florentine,
>
> A fellow almost damned in a fair wife;
>
> That never set a squadron in the field,
>
> Nor the division of a battle knows
>
> More than a spinster – unless the bookish theoric,
>
> Wherein the toged consuls can propose
>
> As masterly as he. Mere prattle without practice,
>
> Is all his soldiership

(a) What is the dramatic significance of Iago delivering this verdict?

....

....

(b) How far do you think there is any truth in Iago's view of Cassio?

....

....

CONTINUED ➡

4   Read from Cassio's 'Tempests themselves ...' to his 'Enwheel thee round' (2.1.68–87).

    What do Cassio's words reveal about (a) his attitude towards Desdemona, and (b) his social background?

    ....

    ....

    ....

    ....

5   How far do you think social context is a factor in Cassio's different attitudes towards Desdemona and Bianca?

    ....

    ....

    ....

    ....

6   Read the following complaint by Roderigo to Iago (2.3.358–64). Then write a paragraph explaining how far you sympathise with Roderigo, here and elsewhere in the play, and why.

> I do follow here in the chase not like a hound that hunts, but one that fills up the cry. My money is almost spent, I have been tonight exceedingly well cudgelled, and I think the issue will be I shall have so much experience for my pains: and so, with no money at all, and a little more wit, return again to Venice.

    ....

    ....

    ....

    ....

    ....

    ....

TAKING IT FURTHER

7   'Cassio is a worthy successor to Othello, and at the end of the play Cyprus is safe in his hands.' Plan and write a 500-word essay evaluating this statement.

Challenge yourself

The role of Roderigo is rather like that of Sir Andrew Aguecheek in the Shakespeare comedy *Twelfth Night*. Sir Andrew is a fool tricked into challenging Sebastian, whom he wrongs and expects to be a feeble coward. Does this remind you of anyone in *Othello*? How far do you see Roderigo as a comic character?

Brabantio and minor characters

STARTING OUT

1   Brabantio is not developed into a fully rounded character. Add to the spidergram below to suggest ways in which he is nonetheless important to the plot.

Warns ...

Contradictory attitudes to Othello

Brabantio

2   How is Brabantio's warning to Othello significant in terms of Othello's later decline?

....

....

DEVELOPING YOUR IDEAS

3   How does Brabantio help in Shakespeare's presentation of Othello as an outsider?

....

....

4   (a) How does Lodovico influence our attitude to Othello in Act 4, scene 1 line 241 to the end of the scene?

....

....

(b) How are Ludovico's comments here important in terms of the context of the period?

....

....

TAKING IT FURTHER

5　Brabantio is like a number of fathers of daughters in Shakespeare plays. Find out about at least one of the following:

- Capulet, Juliet's father in *Romeo and Juliet*
- Shylock, Jessica's father in *The Merchant of Venice*
- Polonius, Ophelia's father in *Hamlet*
- Prospero, Miranda's father in *The Tempest*.

How are they similar to Brabantio?

6　Write a paragraph explaining how a Shakespearean audience would have viewed Brabantio differently from a modern one.

....

....

....

....

....

....

Writer's methods: language and style

You will enjoy *Othello* more and get higher marks if you can analyse Shakespeare's language. For example, animal imagery hints at the lower aspects of human nature. Othello uses it more as he sinks into jealousy. At the same time, his language becomes less stately and more erratic, reflecting his emotional state.

STARTING OUT

1   Identify the speaker of each quotation and give your view of how its *language* shows their personality, or their mood at that point in the play. For example, it might show a particular attitude towards the opposite sex, or a playful mood, or emotional disturbance.

LINE(S)	CHARACTER	WHAT IT SHOWS
A Most potent, grave, and reverend signiors,/ My very noble and approved good masters		
B Were they [Desdemona and Cassio] as prime as goats, as hot as monkeys,/ As salt as wolves in pride		
C Pish! Noses, ears, and lips. Is't possible? Confess! handkerchief! O devil!		
D he hath achieved a maid/ That paragons description and wild fame;/ One that excels the quirks of blazoning pens		
E Why, this is not a boon,/ 'Tis as I should entreat you wear your gloves,/ Or feed on nourishing dishes		

CONTINUED ➔

    Answers can be found at: www.hoddereducation.co.uk/workbookanswers

2   Match each line below to the literary technique of which it is an example, and evaluate its effect on audiences. Choose from:

metaphor   simile   personification   rhetorical question   alliteration   parallelism

(a) Iago: It is the green-eyed monster, which doth mock/ The meat it feeds on.

....

....

....

(b) Desdemona: Shall I deny you?

....

....

....

(c) Othello: She loved me for the dangers I had passed/ And I loved her that she did pity them.

....

....

....

(d) Iago: the thought whereof/ Doth like a poisonous mineral gnaw my inwards

....

....

....

(e) Iago: The food that to him now is as luscious as locusts

....

....

....

(f) Othello: I will a round unvarnished tale deliver

....

....

....

KEY SKILLS

Using literary terminology

Weave your identification of a technique into the sentence in which you analyse its effect.

Example: 'The simile in which Iago compares the thought of Othello sleeping with Emilia to "a poisonous mineral" gnawing at his insides suggests that he really does suffer from this belief.'

DEVELOPING YOUR IDEAS

3 Read the Key Skills box above. Then write similar sentences evaluating the effects of three more of the quotations in **Activity 2**.

(a) ....

....

(b) ....

....

(c) ....

....

4 Divide the following images into three main types according to their content. For example, some are images of *poison or disease*. Where two types are combined, choose which you think is the dominant one.

A you'll have your daughter covered [mated] with a Barbary horse

B Dangerous conceits are in their natures poisons ... Burn like the mines of sulphur.

C Even then this forked plague is fated to us/ When we do quicken.

D prime as goats, as hot as monkeys,/ As salt as wolves

E Will you, I pray, demand that demi-devil/ Why he hath thus ensnared my soul and body?

F I must show out a flag and sign of love

G With as little a web as this will I ensnare as great a fly as Cassio.

H ... out of her goodness make the net/ That shall enmesh them all.

I I had rather be a toad/ And live upon the vapour of a dungeon

Type 1: Poison or disease

Examples: ....

Type 2: ....

Examples: ....

Type 3: ....

Examples: ....

5   Circle the best words in the options below to complete the two paragraphs.

Images of poison or [hunger/disease/darkness/trickery] are appropriate to *Othello*

because of the way that Iago gradually [discovers/dilutes/corrupts/steals] Othello's

noble nature and the [forbidden/pure/explosive/enduring] love between him and

Desdemona. Iago comments that 'Dangerous conceits' – damaging false imaginings – are,

[metaphorically/literally/roughly/accurately] speaking, 'poisons' that infect the blood.

The vivid [personification/simile/metaphor/oxymoron] Iago uses, picturing them as

burning 'the blood ... like the mines of sulphur' is effectively unpleasant, especially because

sulphur was [associated/manufactured/mixed/compared] with hellfire.

6   Annotate these speeches spoken by Othello to show how his rhetorical language makes him seem dramatic and exotic.

   (a)

> I ran it through, even from my boyish days
> To th' very moment that he bade me tell it,
> Wherein I spake of most disastrous chances,
> Of moving accidents by flood and field,
> Of hair-breadth scapes i'th' imminent deadly breach,
> Of being taken by the insolent foe
> And sold to slavery; of my redemption thence
> And portance in my travailous history;
> Wherein of antres vast and deserts idle,
> Rough quarries, rocks and hills whose heads touch heaven
> It was my hint to speak – such was my process –
> And of the cannibals that each other eat,
> The Anthropophagi, and men whose heads
> Do grow beneath their shoulders.
> (1.3.133–46)

Rhetorical: describing language that uses particular techniques to persuade or have a dramatic impact.

CONTINUED ➡

(b)

> O now, for ever
>
> Farewell the tranquil mind, farewell content!
>
> Farewell the plumed troops and the big wars
>
> That make ambition virtue! O farewell,
>
> Farewell the neighing steed and the shrill trump,
>
> The spirit-stirring drum, the ear-piercing fife,
>
> The royal banner, and all quality,
>
> Pride, pomp and circumstance of glorious war!
>
> And, O you mortal engines whose rude throats
>
> Th' immortal Jove's dread clamours counterfeit,
>
> Farewell: Othello's occupation's gone!
>
> (3.3.350–60)

7 (a) What do you think is the additional practical purpose of these two speeches in terms of Shakespeare's stagecraft?

....

....

....

....

(b) How might a modern audience view each of these two speeches differently from a Jacobean one?

....

....

....

....

....

....

....

KEY SKILLS

Analysing language

You will gain credit for close analysis of the impact of Shakespeare's language choices, including accurate and relevant use of technical terms.

TAKING IT FURTHER

8   Read the two student comments below on types of imagery in *Othello*. Which do you find more effective and why? Find at least two strengths or weaknesses in each one.

A   Shakespeare uses animal imagery throughout the play to hint at the lower, bestial part of human nature. Early on it is voiced by Iago, as in his provocative assertion to Brabantio, '… an old black ram/ Is tupping your white ewe!'. This metaphor, picturing Othello and Desdemona as mating sheep, reduces even marital sex to the level of animal breeding. It also implies that Othello is animalistic in his desires.

B   Iago is sick and wants to make Othello sick too. 'I'll pour this pestilence into his ear.' Pestilence is a kind of disease they had a lot in Shakespeare's day. Iago basically wants to mess with Othello's mind by pouring in pestilence. It shows that Iago is full of ill will towards Othello and that Othello has no idea what is going on. Pouring makes it sound dead easy.

A   Strengths: ....

....

Weaknesses: ....

....

B   Strengths: ....

....

Weaknesses: ....

....

9   Now choose one of the other types of image from **Activity 4** and write a paragraph analysing how that type of image fits with the themes of the play. Remember to use short, well-selected quotations to illustrate your points. You could include the way in which Shakespeare sometimes combines two types of image for greater impact.

....

....

....

....

....

....

....

....

CONTINUED ➡

10 Read, annotate and compare the two speeches below. Then write a paragraph comparing their language and dramatic effect. Othello's speech leads up to his vowing vengeance and making his pact with Iago. Lady Macbeth's speech is spoken when she is preparing herself for the murder of King Duncan.

Othello	**Lady Macbeth**
Look here, Iago;	Come, you spirits
All my fond love thus do I blow to heaven:	That tend on mortal thoughts, unsex me here,
'Tis gone!	And fill me from the crown to the toe top-full
Arise, black vengeance, from the hollow hell,	Of direst cruelty! Make thick my blood;
Yield up, O love, thy crown and hearted throne	Stop up the access and passage to remorse,
To tyrannous hate! Swell, bosom, with thy fraught,	That no compunctious visitings of nature
For 'tis of aspics' tongues!	Shake my fell purpose, nor keep peace between
(*Othello*, 3.3.447–53)	The effect and it!
	(*Macbeth*, 1.5.40–7)

....

....

....

....

....

....

....

KEY SKILLS

Interpreting images

Analysing imagery is not an exact science. You will gain credit for your own interpretation of an image's effect, providing you make a persuasive case.

11 Read this extract from a high-level student essay analysing Iago's persuasive language and its impact on Othello.

Annotate the response A–F to show the strengths listed below. (A strength may be shown more than once.)

A accurate uses of literary terminology

B fluently embedded quotations

C effective references to language without direct quotation

D effective analysis of language

E comparison with another text

F exploration of critical views

We see how much Iago's insulting picture of Cassio wiping his beard with Desdemona's handkerchief inflames Othello's hatred for Cassio by the hyperbole of his wish to kill him forty thousand times over. The line 'Now do I see 'tis true' shows that Othello is finally convinced, so that he makes a ritual of blowing his foolish love to heaven. Now we see how far he has been corrupted by Iago: he summons 'black vengeance' from hell in preparation for killing Desdemona, and replaces all his love with hate. His language can be compared with that of Lady Macbeth, in *Macbeth*, when she calls on spirits to take away her femininity so that she can help to murder King Duncan. Othello's image of 'aspics' tongues' gives us a sense of the poisonous, murderous and bestial urges that he now feels, as does, in a more earthy way, the repetition 'O blood, blood, blood!'

Iago's pretended attempt to calm Othello reinforces his credibility while actually stirring Othello up even more. His extended simile comparing his murderous determination to the one-way tide of the Pontic Sea is terrifying in its icy power. It also hints at the self-dramatising tendency that some critics (such as Leavis and Wilson Knight) have seen in Othello's speeches. He is comparing himself to a mighty ocean.

CONTINUED ➡

The vow which Othello grandly makes 'by yond marble heaven' both suggests a coldness of purpose which will enable him to steel his passion to effective action, and shows his fixed determination now that he is finally convinced. Iago's kneeling beside him to make his own vow is a master-stroke of dramatic ingenuity, calculated to make Othello see Iago as the one man truly on his side. Iago heightens the effect by imitating Othello's grandiose appeal to cosmic forces.

12 On a separate sheet, write a similar analysis of Iago's persuasive language and Roderigo's response in the passage from Iago's 'It is merely a lust of the blood ...' to Roderigo's exit (1.3.335–81). Consider Iago's use of rhetorical techniques, such as:

- repetition
- alliteration
- imagery
- emotive word choices.

Challenge yourself

Read the speech in which Othello makes his vow of revenge (3.3.455–65). How does Othello's language match his intention here? How does Iago make his language in the next speech ape Othello's? Why does he do this?

Contexts

You should be aware of the text as a product of its historical, social and cultural context, and how audiences have interpreted the text over time, up to the present day.

To gain credit for AO5 you will have to show an awareness of relevant context, incorporating references in your response where appropriate.

> **KEY SKILLS**
>
> **Incorporating context**
>
> You should find that if you answer the question fully then you will be including context. You should not add unintegrated references to context as an afterthought.

Historical and social context

STARTING OUT

1 *Othello* is set in about 1570, when the Turks were attempting to take the strategically important Mediterranean island of Cyprus, at that point held by the Venetian Republic.

Read Act 1, scene 3, up to Brabantio's entry (line 48). Then answer these questions:

(a) How does the situation in which the Duke of Venice and his senators find themselves create an appropriate setting for the emotional events of the play?

....

....

....

(b) How exactly does the Turkish fleet behave and how does this correspond to the action of the play?

....

....

....

(c) How does the situation seem to work to Othello's advantage?

....

....

....

CONTINUED ➡

2 Acts 2–5 are set in Cyprus, which is a frontier garrison threatened by the Turks. Cyprus is Christian, the Turks Muslim. To Shakespeare's audience, only the Christian world was civilised. They would also know that shortly after the time of the play, Cyprus was captured by the Turks and remained under Turkish rule. Suggest how this might parallel what happens to Othello in the play.

   ....

   ....

   ....

3 (a) Circle words and phrases below that you think could refer to important elements of *Othello*'s social context.

   | Poverty | War | Gender | Class | Exploration | Racism |

   | Science | Honour and reputation | Education |

   (b) Take three of your circled contexts and suggest for each how it would have influenced perceptions of the play in Shakespeare's time, and how it might influence audiences now.

CONTEXT	THEN	NOW
1		
2		
3		

CONTINUED

Answers can be found at: www.hoddereducation.co.uk/workbookanswers

4 Look up the quotations below and explain how each relates to social or historical context. The first has been done for you.

LINE	CONTEXT
A Iago: ... the devil will make a grandsire of you (1.1.90)	This shows religious belief, a racist identification of Othello with the devil, and a father's assumed right to choose his daughter's husband.
B Brabantio: It is a judgement maimed and most imperfect That will confess perfection so could err Against all rules of nature, and must be driven To find out practices of cunning hell (1.3.100–4)	
C Brabantio: Do you perceive, in all this noble company, Where most you owe obedience? (1.3.179–80)	
D Cassio: Let it not gall your patience, good Iago, That I extend my manners; 'tis my breeding That gives me this bold show of courtesy. (2.1.97–9)	
E Iago: Good name in man and woman, dear my lord, Is the immediate jewel of their souls (3.3.158–9)	

CONTINUED ➡

F Othello: A horned man's a monster, and a beast. (4.1.62)	
G Othello: ... so delicate with a needle, an admirable musician. O, she will sing the savageness out of a bear! (4.1.184–5)	
H Othello: Where a malignant and a turbanned Turk Beat a Venetian and traduced the state, I took by th' throat the circumcised dog (5.2.351–3)	

DEVELOPING YOUR IDEAS

5   How successful do you think the following student paragraph is in incorporating social context into its argument?

Annotate it to show its strength and weaknesses. Then write an overall assessment.

> Desdemona is presented as a pure, virtuous teenage girl who accepts the conventional Jacobean belief that wives should be entirely faithful to their husbands, even if husbands are unfaithful. She even doubts that 'there be women do abuse their husbands/ In such gross kind', referring to adultery. She swears 'by this heavenly light' that she would not, linking fidelity to Christian obedience, but perhaps also to Diana, goddess of chastity and of the moon, if 'light' refers to the moon here.

Your assessment:

....

....

....

....

CONTINUED ➡

Answers can be found at: www.hoddereducation.co.uk/workbookanswers

6 The paragraph from a student essay below misses several opportunities to weave in relevant social and historical context. Rewrite it, making the relevance of context clear.

Othello is an outsider, as indicated by his being often referred to simply as 'the Moor'. As a mercenary, he is useful to the state, and he appears to have been welcome in Brabantio's home, but Brabantio does not want him to marry Desdemona, and thinks Othello must have won her trust by trickery. Desdemona has shown boldness in marrying Othello.

....

....

....

....

....

....

....

....

....

....

....

....

....

7 Consider this statement:

'Throughout the play, Desdemona plays the role of passive victim, even to the point of being partly to blame for the tragedy.'

Make notes below on how social context could be relevant to the following elements in the play if you were writing a response on how far you agree with this statement on Desdemona.

(a) Desdemona's marriage

....

....

....

(b) Her desire to go to Cyprus with Othello

....

....

....

CONTINUED ➡

(c) Her efforts on Cassio's behalf

....

....

....

(d) Her refusal to believe that Othello could be jealous

....

....

....

(e) Her reaction when Othello strikes her

....

....

....

(f) How she dies.

....

....

....

TAKING IT FURTHER

8   Read the following two passages:
- Act 3, scene 4, line 169 (Bianca's entry) to the end of the scene
- Act 4, scene 1, lines 109–62 ('Alas, poor caitiff' to 'Faith, I intend so').

On a separate sheet, plan and write a response to the following question, referring to relevant context:

How does Shakespeare's presentation of Cassio and Bianca in these passages reveal their characters?

KEY SKILLS

Writing about characters

Do not make the mistake of writing about the characters as if they are real people. Remember that they are Shakespeare's dramatic constructions and write about them as such, showing *how* he presents them – what techniques he uses.

Challenge yourself

Bianca's name means 'White'. How far do you think Shakespeare's naming of her is ironic, and how far do you think he means to defend her by calling her this? Is she really a courtesan – a high-class prostitute – or is this just how men perceive her?

Cultural context

1 For each cultural concept or belief below, suggest at least one way in which it features in *Othello*.

(a) The Chain of Being – a hierarchical order of beings, whose breakdown leads to Chaos

....

....

....

(b) Nature – the idea that social well-being depends on 'natural' behaviour

....

....

....

(c) The importance of reason to humanity

....

....

....

(d) Belief in evil and damnation

....

....

....

(e) Belief in the importance of honesty

....

....

....

(f) Courtly love

....

....

....

(g) Male fear of being cuckolded

....

....

....

DEVELOPING YOUR IDEAS

2   Add notes around the quotations below on how they relate to cultural concepts or beliefs.

(a) Othello:

> Sweet soul, take heed,
>
> Take heed of perjury. Thou art on thy death-bed.
>
> (5.2.50–1)

(b) Othello:

> perdition catch my soul,
>
> But I do love thee! and when I love thee not
>
> Chaos is come again.
>
> (3.3.90–2)

(c) Cassio:

> You men of Cyprus, let her have your knees!
>
> Hail to thee, lady, and the grace of heaven,
>
> Before, behind thee, and on every hand
>
> Enwheel thee round!
>
> (2.1.84–7)

(d) Othello:

> It is not words that shakes me thus. Pish! Noses, ears, and lips.
> Is't possible? Confess! handkerchief! O devil!
>
> (4.1.41–3)

CONTINUED ➡

3 Make notes on how honest each of these characters is regarded as being by other characters in the play, and how honest each actually is:

(a) Othello

....

....

(b) Iago

....

....

(c) Desdemona

....

....

(d) Emilia

....

....

(e) Cassio

....

....

TAKING IT FURTHER

4 Bearing cultural context in mind, write at least one paragraph explaining how far you agree with one or both of these statements:

(a) Othello's marriage upsets the social order, which ultimately leads to tragedy.

(b) Othello's great mistake is to trust Iago, his subordinate, rather than his own wife.

....

....

....

....

....

....

....

....

Critical approaches

There is no single correct interpretation of any Shakespeare play, or any character. To receive marks for AO5 it is important to consider alternative interpretations of *Othello*, including your own. One way to approach this is through looking at broad schools of criticism and at individual critics.

STARTING OUT

1   What do you see as the play's key critical controversies? Add your ideas below. One has been done for you.

Othello	Iago
	• Does he have motives?
	• If so, what are they?
	• Is he a realistic character or a plot device?

Desdemona	Cassio

How Shakespeare presents women	How Shakespeare presents race.

CONTINUED ➜

Answers can be found at: www.hoddereducation.co.uk/workbookanswers

KEY SKILLS

Evaluating criticism

Try to evaluate any critics or broad schools of criticism you cite: use them to build on your own ideas.

---

2 Read Othello's farewell speech below. Annotate the extract to give your own views to the questions at the bottom of the page relating to the underlined words and phrases.

> Soft you, a word or two before you go.
>
> I have done the state some service, and they know't:
>
> <u>No more of that.</u>[1] I pray you, in your letters,
>
> When you shall these <u>unlucky deeds</u>[2] relate,
>
> Speak of me as I am. Nothing extenuate,
>
> Nor set down aught in malice. Then must you speak
>
> Of one that loved <u>not wisely, but too well;</u>[3]
>
> Of one <u>not easily jealous,</u>[4] but, being wrought,
>
> Perplexed in the extreme; of one whose hand,
>
> Like the base Indian, threw <u>a pearl</u>[5] away
>
> Richer than all his tribe; of one whose subdued eyes,
>
> Albeit unused to the melting mood,
>
> <u>Drops tears as fast as the Arabian trees</u>
>
> <u>Their medicinable gum.</u>[6] Set you down this,
>
> And say besides that <u>in Aleppo once,</u>
>
> <u>Where a malignant and a turbanned Turk</u>
>
> <u>Beat a Venetian and traduced the state,</u>
>
> <u>I took by th' throat the circumcised dog</u>[7]
>
> And smote him – thus!
>
> (5.2.335-53)

1 Does he mean, 'I will say no more about that' or 'I will not serve the state anymore'?
2 Is he denying responsibility by calling Desdemona's death bad luck?
3 How do you interpret 'not wisely'? Is his self-image accurate?
4 True?
5 What could this refer to, and what does his simile suggest?
6 Why this choice of image?
7 A clever lead up to suicide? What other agendas might he (or Shakespeare) have?

CONTINUED ➡

DEVELOPING YOUR IDEAS

While it is possible to distinguish broad schools of thought in Shakespeare criticism, you should be wary of making sweeping statements such as, 'Feminist criticism would see Desdemona as a passive victim of patriarchal forces.' It is more useful to begin with the aspects of the play that might be of special interest to a school of critical thought, and to develop your own ideas from there.

3 Match each critical viewpoint to its defining characteristics and a quotation in which critics of that school might be especially interested.

CRITICAL VIEWPOINT	CHARACTERISTICS	REFERENCE
(a) New historicism	1 Viewing a text as a reflection of the socio-political conditions in which it was produced, especially in terms of class and power.	A Iago: Even now, now, very now, an old black ram Is tupping your white ewe! (1.1.87–8)
(b) Feminist criticism	2 Sees the text as a product of its historical, social and cultural context.	B Othello: Lie with her? lie on her? We say lie on her when they belie her! Lie with her, zounds, that's fulsome!! – Handkerchief! confessions! handkerchief! (4.1.35–7)
(c) Post-colonial criticism	3 Sees the text as expressing repressed desires and the conflict between them and social expectations, especially shown in symbolism.	C Othello: Where a malignant and a turbanned Turk Beat a Venetian and traduced the state, I took by th' throat the circumcised dog … (5.2.351–3)
(d) Psychoanalytical criticism	4 Questioning evidence of patriarchal ideology and misogyny.	D Lodovico: You must forsake this room, and go with us. Your power and your command is taken off, And Cassio rules in Cyprus. (5.2.328–30)
(e) Marxist criticism	5 Focuses on the presentation of ethnic minorities, especially on their exploitation.	E Cassio: 'Tis such another fitchew; marry, a perfumed one. What do you mean by this haunting of me? (4.1.145–6)

CONTINUED

Answers can be found at: www.hoddereducation.co.uk/workbookanswers

4 How do you think a critic from each of the schools in **Activity 3** would regard the quotation with which you have linked it?

CRITICAL VIEWPOINT	POSSIBLE INTERPRETATION
(a) New historicism	
(b) Feminist criticism	
(c) Post-colonial criticism	
(d) Psychoanalytical criticism	
(e) Marxist criticism	

5 What other interpretations could apply to the quotations above? Consider other schools of criticism and try to develop your own ideas. Add your own interpretations to the table below.

REFERENCE	YOUR INTERPRETATION
A Iago: Even now, now, very now, an old black ram Is tupping your white ewe! (1.1.87–8)	
B Othello: Lie with her? lie on her? We say lie on her when they belie her! Lie with her, zounds, that's fulsome! – Handkerchief! confessions! handkerchief! (4.1.35–7)	
C Othello: Where a malignant and a turbanned Turk Beat a Venetian and traduced the state, I took by th' throat the circumcised dog (5.2.351–3)	

CONTINUED →

D Lodovico: You must forsake this room, and go with us. Your power and your command is taken off, And Cassio rules in Cyprus. (5.2.328–30)	
E Cassio: 'Tis such another fitchew; marry, a perfumed one. What do you mean by this haunting of me? (4.1.145–6)	

6   Refer back to **Activity 2**. TS Eliot comments on Othello's speech:

> What Othello seems to me to be doing in making this speech is *cheering himself up*. He is endeavouring to escape reality, he has ceased to think about Desdemona, and is thinking about himself.
>
> (Selected Essays, 1932)

How far do you agree with Eliot's view? Make notes either on paper or on your copy of the play to support your ideas.

CONTINUED

TAKING IT FURTHER

Take your critical interpretation further by reading the work of individual critics. If you quote or refer to critics' ideas in the exam, acknowledge them, integrate them into your own argument and use them to develop your own interpretations.

7   Read the views of the critics below. Add your own view in the central rectangle.

Thomas Rymer, A Short View of Tragedy (1693)	Your view	Karen Newman, 'Femininity and the Monstrous in *Othello*' (1991)
'So much ado, so much stress, so much passion and repetition about an Handkerchief! Why was this not called the *Tragedy of the Handkerchief?* ... Had it been Desdemona's Garter, the Sagacious Moor might have smelt a Rat; but the Handkerchief is so remote a trifle, no Booby on this side of Mauritania could make any consequence of it.'	....	'The handkerchief in *Othello* is what we might term a snowballing signifier, for as it passes from hand to hand, both literal and critical, it accumulates myriad associations and meanings. ... The handkerchief, with its associations with the mother, witchcraft, and the marvellous, represents the link between femininity and the monstrous which Othello and Desdemona's union figures in the play.'

CONTINUED ➔

8 Some critics' views become so well-known that it is tempting to take it for granted that they are correct.

Samuel Taylor Coleridge famously spoke of Iago's final soliloquy in Act 1 as 'the motive-hunting of motiveless malignity', encouraging the view that Iago has no real motives and, therefore, simply enjoys causing harm for its own sake.

How convincing do you find this view? What evidence to the contrary can you find in this soliloquy and in the play as a whole?

....

....

....

....

....

....

....

Challenge yourself

Lynda E Boose in 'The Pornographic Aesthetic of *Othello*' finds evidence of voyeurism in the play:

Iago plays the pander who opens the door to the listener's pornographic imagination. ... Far more than a genuine 'character' with discernibly coherent motivation, Iago is a role, a strategy within the *Othello* text that shapes the play's construction.

How far do you agree with this viewpoint?

Boosting your skills

Whichever exam board you are studying for, you will benefit from considering all the exam-style questions in this section.

Fulfilling the Assessment Objectives

The headings in this section include the particular AOs relevant to each subsection. In your exam response it is best to attempt to cover all the AOs by answering the question fully, rather than adding something just to cover a particular AO. However, it will help you to keep the AOs in mind in order to improve your ability to answer fully.

1   Add notes beneath each AO below on what you think each one means and what it includes, with examples.

●   AO1: Articulate informed, personal and creative responses to literary texts, using associated concepts and terminology, and coherent, accurate written expression.

....

....

●   AO2: Analyse ways in which meanings are shaped in literary texts.

....

....

●   AO3: Demonstrate understanding of the significance and influence of the contexts in which literary texts are written and received.

....

....

●   AO4: Explore connections across literary texts.

....

....

●   AO5: Explore literary texts informed by different interpretations.

....

....

....

Preparing to answer the question (AO1)

A successful exam response starts with reading the question properly and considering how to answer it.

2   Read the passage below. Then read the AQA (A) type question that follows it, and annotate the passage to help you prepare to answer it.

This to hear

Would Desdemona seriously incline,

But still the house affairs would draw her thence,

CONTINUED ➔

Which ever as she could with haste dispatch

She'd come again, and with a greedy ear

Devour up my discourse; which I, observing,

Took once a pliant hour and found good means

To draw from her a prayer of earnest heart

That I would all my pilgrimage dilate,

Whereof by parcels she had something heard

But not intentively. I did consent,

And often did beguile her of her tears

When I did speak of some distressful stroke

That my youth suffered. My story being done

She gave me for my pains a world of sighs,

She swore in faith 'twas strange, 'twas passing strange,

'Twas pitiful, 'twas wondrous pitiful;

She wished she had not heard it, yet she wished

That heaven had made her such a man. She thanked me

And bade me, if I had a friend that loved her,

I should but teach him how to tell my story

And that would woo her. Upon this hint I spake:

She loved me for the dangers I had passed,

And I loved her that she did pity them.

This only is the witchcraft I have used:

Enter DESDEMONA, IAGO, *Attendants.*

Here comes the lady; let her witness it.

DUKE	I think this tale would win my daughter too.
	Good Brabantio, take up this mangled matter at the best:
	Men do their broken weapons rather use
	Than their bare hands.
BRABANTIO	I pray you, hear her speak.
	If she confess that she was half the wooer,
	Destruction on my head if my bad blame
	Light on the man. Come hither, gentle mistress:
	Do you perceive, in all this noble company,
	Where most you owe obedience?

CONTINUED

> DESDEMONA   My noble father,
>
>   I do perceive here a divided duty.
>
>   To you I am bound for life and education:
>
>   My life and education both do learn me
>
>   How to respect you; you are the lord of duty,
>
>   I am hitherto your daughter. But here's my husband:
>
>   And so much duty as my mother showed
>
>   To you, preferring you before her father,
>
>   So much I challenge that I may profess
>
>   Due to the Moor my lord.
>
>   (1.3.146–89)

- How does Shakespeare present aspects of love in this passage?
- Consider the view that, as shown by this passage and the play as a whole, the marriage of Othello and Desdemona is ill-founded and therefore doomed.

(a) Make brief notes identifying four aspects of love in this passage.

....

....

....

....

(b) Underline what you think are the key words in the second bullet point.

(c) In the table below, make notes on how the passage suggests that the marriage is 'ill-founded' and arguments to the contrary. One note has been added for you.

ILL-FOUNDED	SOUND BASIS FOR MARRIAGE
Desdemona's attraction based on Othello's version of himself and his life.	

CONTINUED ➤

3   Read the extract below. Then read the AQA (B) type question that follows it and annotate the extract to help you answer it.

IAGO   Tell me but this,

Have you not sometimes seen a handkerchief

Spotted with strawberries, in your wife's hand?

OTHELLO   I gave her such a one, 'twas my first gift.

IAGO   I know not that, but such a handkerchief,

I am sure it was your wife's, did I today

See Cassio wipe his beard with.

OTHELLO   If it be that –

IAGO   If it be that, or any that was hers,

It speaks against her with the other proofs.

OTHELLO   O that the slave had forty thousand lives!

One is too poor, too weak for my revenge.

Now do I see 'tis true. Look here, Iago,

All my fond love thus do I blow to heaven:

'Tis gone!

Arise, black vengeance, from the hollow hell!

Yield up, O love, thy crown and hearted throne

To tyrannous hate! Swell, bosom, with thy fraught,

For 'tis of aspics' tongues!

IAGO   Yet be content.

OTHELLO   O, blood, blood, blood!

Othello kneels.

IAGO   Patience, I say, your mind perhaps may change.

OTHELLO   Never, Iago. Like to the Pontic sea,

Whose icy current and compulsive course

Ne'er keeps retiring ebb but keeps due on

To the Propontic and the Hellespont:

Even so my bloody thoughts with violent pace

Shall ne'er look back, ne'er ebb to humble love

Till that a capable and wide revenge

Swallow them up. Now by yond marble heaven

CONTINUED ➡

In the due reverence of a sacred vow

I here engage my words.

IAGO   Do not rise yet.

Iago kneels.

Witness, you ever–burning lights above,

You elements that clip us round about,

Witness that here Iago doth give up

The execution of his wit, hands, heart,

To wronged Othello's service! Let him command

And to obey shall be in me remorse

What bloody business ever.

OTHELLO   I greet thy love

Not with vain thanks but with acceptance bounteous,

And will upon the instant put thee to't.

Within these three days let me hear thee say

That Cassio's not alive.

IAGO   My friend is dead,

'Tis done – at your request. But let her live.

OTHELLO   Damn her, lewd minx: O, damn her, damn her!

Come, go with me apart; I will withdraw

To furnish me with some swift means of death

For the fair devil. Now art thou my lieutenant.

IAGO   I am your own for ever.

Exeunt

(3.3.436–81)

Now consider this AQA (B) type question:

Explore the significance of aspects of dramatic tragedy in the following passage in relation to the play as a whole.

You should consider the following in your answer:

- how the two characters interact
- the language used by both men
- other relevant aspects of dramatic tragedy.

(a) On a separate sheet of plain paper, produce a concept map or spidergram with the initial branches labelled 'interact', 'language' and 'aspects'. Use this to explore possible points to make in this essay based on this passage. You could consider:
  - how Iago manipulates Othello and how credulous Othello is
  - Othello's use of highly dramatic language and Iago's parody of it
  - how the audience is prepared for what is to come.

CONTINUED ➡

(b) Now, thinking of the whole play, make notes on:
  – one or more other scenes showing Iago's power to manipulate and Othello's credulity

....

....

....

....

....

  – other examples of Othello's self-dramatisation.

....

....

....

....

....

4   Read this Edexcel style question:

Explore how Shakespeare presents relationships between the sexes in Othello. You must relate your discussion to relevant contextual factors and ideas from your critical reading.

(a) Make notes on how you could use the three following scenes to answer this question.
  – Desdemona's 'Why do you speak so startlingly and rash?' to Emilia's 'They belch us.' (3.4.81–107)

....

....

....

....

....

  – Bianca's 'Save you, friend Cassio!' (3.4.169) to the end of the scene

....

....

....

....

CONTINUED ➔

....

....

    – Emilia's 'I am glad I have found this napkin,' to her exit (3.3.294–322)

....

....

....

....

....

....

(b) Make notes on what contextual factors you could include in your essay that relate to these passages. Bear in mind especially:
- each woman's attitude towards her husband or lover, and towards a woman's role generally
- the men's attitude towards the women
- the importance of the handkerchief (napkin), especially to Othello.

....

....

....

....

....

....

CONTINUED ➡

Structuring your essay (AO1)

Planning is the next important stage of your response. AO1 includes the structure of your essay. You need to present your arguments in a logical order, leading to your conclusion.

5   The points below represent one possible plan for a response to the question in **Activity 2**, repeated here for your convenience.

Read from Othello's 'This to hear …' to Desdemona's 'Due to the Moor my lord' (1.3.146–89).

- How does Shakespeare present aspects of love in this passage?
- Consider the view that, as shown by this passage and the play as a whole, the marriage of Othello and Desdemona is ill-founded and therefore doomed.

(a) As this is a passage-based question, the points below are given simply as they appear in the passage, and then followed by those relating to the whole play. How would you arrange them in a logical order that a reader could easily follow, and that better integrates both parts of the question?

A   Desdemona's domestic duties interrupt her listening.   ....

B   'greedy ear/ Devour' – Karen Newman says this shows women as insatiable.   ....

C   'That heaven had made her such a man' ambiguous.   ....

D   Her hint 'if I had a friend' – not as innocent as she seems?   ....

E   Desdemona wants to be man – imagines herself in Othello's adventures?   ....

F   She believes his version of himself.   ....

G   Othello loves her for her compassion.   ....

H   Desdemona is bold and rebellious to marry Othello.   ....

I   Desdemona transfers her obedience from father to husband, her 'lord'.   ....

J   Couple have limited knowledge of each other, or the opposite sex.   ....

K   More knowledge than most couples of the time, and they do fall in love.   ....

(b) Add a note on one or more ways in which you could conclude this essay.

....

....

....

....

CONTINUED

Answers can be found at: www.hoddereducation.co.uk/workbookanswers

6   Now consider this question, which relates to the whole play:

Explore the view that the female characters in Othello are only of secondary importance.

Organise the points below into a coherent plan for answering this question. Aim for a plan that will explore both sides of the question and then reach a conclusion that does not simply opt for one or the other.

A   Dramatic role of women.   ....

B   Handkerchief a symbol of women's role.   ....

C   Main focus is on men, and Othello's transformation.   ....

D   Male attitudes to women in the play.   ....

E   Male imagery.   ....

F   Plot male-driven.   ....

G   Social and historical context.   ....

H   Strength of female characters.   ....

7   Discourse markers, such as 'moreover' or 'however', make your argument easier to follow. Add suitable markers to this response, changing sentence punctuation where necessary.

> Desdemona is often regarded as passive. She fails to defend herself effectively against Othello's outrageous and unfounded accusations, or against her murder. Earlier in the play she is far more proactive. She is bold and rebellious in secretly marrying a man of whom her father will not approve. She respectfully tells Brabantio, in front of the Senate, that her first duty is now towards her husband, her new 'lord'.
>
> Desdemona's spirited independence gets her into trouble when she insists on pleading for Cassio, apparently oblivious to Othello's mounting jealousy. She is no match for the forces of perverted patriarchy in the form of Iago and Othello. She succumbs and dies a meek victim, conforming to Emilia's comment that men 'are all but stomachs, and we all but food'.

CONTINUED ➡

A good beginning (AO1)

8   A good essay opening will briefly show engagement with the question, may hint at what is to follow, and will quickly get into making the first major point. Consider the question below, then annotate and comment on the strengths and weaknesses of the openings that follow.

Explore the view that the female characters in *Othello* are only of secondary importance.

(a) I agree entirely that the female characters in Othello, Desdemona, Emilia and Bianca, are only of secondary importance. The men are much more important. This is because Shakespeare's England was a man's world. Unmarried women had to obey their fathers and married women had to obey their husbands. They were oppressed by men. It was like they were men's property, like horses or houses. In this essay I will show that the male characters are much more important.

Your comment

....

....

....

....

(b) The relative importance of male characters, especially Othello and Iago, is in part a product of Jacobean theatre using boy actors for female roles, though it does also reflect the male social dominance of the period. Othello and Iago certainly have more lines than their wives, and it is Iago's decision to torment and ruin Othello that is at the centre of the tragedy. Yet Desdemona is far from being a mere pawn, Emilia is exploited but defiant, and even Bianca shows strength of character in objecting to Cassio's casual treatment of her.

Your comment

....

....

....

....

DEVELOPING YOUR IDEAS

Using textual references (AO1)

It is important to back up your argument with evidence in the form of short quotations or references to precisely identified moments in the text. If you are unsure of the wording, use a single key word, or refer to a passage as follows:

Othello tells Iago that now he is persuaded, his vengeful will is like a mighty ocean that flows in only one direction.

Where possible, embed your quotations:

Iago is deliberately unconvincing when he suggests that the drunken Cassio must have suffered 'some strange indignity' to behave as he did.

9   Make the points given below in your own words, embedding short quotations selected from the longer ones given.

(a) Iago relishes his tormenting of Othello.

> Not poppy, nor mandragora
> Nor all the drowsy syrups of the world
> Shall ever medicine thee to that sweet sleep
> Which thou owedst yesterday.
> (3.3.333-36)

....

....

....

(b) Othello imagines that ignorance would have been bliss.

> I had been happy if the general camp,
> Pioneers and all, had tasted her sweet body,
> So I had nothing known.
> (3.3.348-50)

....

....

....

(c) Iago makes himself seem even more honest by pretending to give up friendship because it leads to honesty.

> O monstrous world! Take note, take note, O world,
> To be direct and honest is not safe.
> I thank you for this profit, and from hence
> I'll love no friend, sith love breeds such offence.
> (3.3.380-83)

....

....

....

CONTINUED ➔

Your conclusion (AO1)

Students often write essays that begin well and develop their argument, but then somehow fail to drive this home in an effective conclusion. One mistake is just to repeat what has already been said; another is to try to introduce a new point at the last moment, when there is no time or space to develop it.

10 Read the following conclusion to a response to the question in **Activity 6** ('Explore the view that the female characters in *Othello* are only of secondary importance.').

> Finally, the play's most powerful symbol – the handkerchief – is feminine. It was made by a prophetess, given by an Egyptian woman to Othello's mother, and it now belongs to Desdemona. Since it is said to have magical power, and is the means by which Iago convinces Othello of Desdemona's guilt, it assumes huge dramatic significance. Thus it provides an appropriate symbol for the role of women in the play. Although of secondary importance in plot progression, they are of equal significance dramatically, as well as showing a different kind of strength within the confines of Jacobean gender roles.

(a) How does this conclusion manage to avoid both pitfalls?

....

....

(b) What other strengths does this conclusion have?

....

....

11 Imagine you have written a response to the essay question above in which you have argued that female characters *are* of secondary importance in the play because of their role in Jacobean society, but that the important dynamic of the play is Iago's domination of his victims. Write an effective conclusion. You could refer back to the question or finish with a short, well-chosen quotation.

....

....

....

....

....

....

....

....

CONTINUED ➡

KEY SKILLS

Be concise

Aim to write in a way that is fluent yet concise. Waffling is often a sign of a candidate who is not sure what they want to say. Do not begin your conclusion with a phrase such as, 'As I believe I have shown convincingly throughout this essay ...'.

Close analysis of the text (AO2)

12 In responding to passage-based questions you will, of course, need to focus closely on the dramatic techniques and language of the passage, and relate the passage to the play as a whole. Imagine you are answering a question on 'aspects of dramatic tragedy', and have been prompted to consider how Iago is presented.

(a) Read and annotate his speech below to show:
- how Shakespeare's language choices show Iago's character
- how the speech engages the audience in Iago's plans
- what it shows about Iago's motives
- how Iago regards himself.

> Go to, farewell, put money enough in your purse.
>
> Thus do I ever make my fool my purse:
>
> For I mine own gained knowledge should profane
>
> If I would time expend with such a snipe
>
> But for my sport and profit. I hate the Moor
>
> And it is thought abroad that 'twixt my sheets
>
> He's done my office. I know not if 't be true,
>
> But I for mere suspicion in that kind
>
> Will do as if for surety. He holds me well,
>
> The better shall my purpose work on him.
>
> Cassio's a proper man: let me see now,
>
> To get his place, and to plume up my will
>
> In double knavery. How? How? Let's see:
>
> After some time to abuse Othello's ear
>
> That he is too familiar with his wife.

CONTINUED ➡

He hath a person and a smooth dispose

To be suspected, framed to make women false.

The Moor is of a free and open nature

That thinks men honest that but seem to be so,

And will as tenderly be led by th' nose

As asses are.

I have't, it is engendered! Hell and night

Must bring this monstrous birth to the world's light.

(b) Using your annotations, write at least one paragraph analysing how this speech shows 'aspects of dramatic tragedy'. Remember to refer closely to the text.

....

....

....

....

....

....

....

....

13 Even when writing about the play as a whole, you will get credit for close analysis of language. Try to weave your analysis into sentences containing your quotations.

Add analysis in the gaps in the following passage:

At first Othello has the .... to tell his accusers, in

Act 1, scene 2, 'Keep up your bright swords.' However, thanks to Iago, he gradually breaks

down, his .... language showing his .... :

'Pish! Noses, ears and lips. Is't possible?' (Act 4, scene 1).

CONTINUED

Answers can be found at: www.hoddereducation.co.uk/workbookanswers

14 Use the notes and hints below to write a fluent paragraph incorporating close analysis of the impact of language.

- The play's imagery is masculine.
- Othello: 'sea-mark of my utmost sail' (Act 5, scene 2). What adjective could you use to describe the semantic field of this image? Is it a simile or a metaphor?
- Iago: 'the net/ That shall enmesh them all' (Act 2, scene 3). How could you classify this image? Is it a simile or a metaphor?
- Iago: 'an old black ram/ Is tupping your white ewe!' (Act 1, scene 1). How could you classify this image? Is it a simile or a metaphor? What is its impact?

....

....

....

....

....

....

....

....

Semantic field: collection of words and phrases relating to a particular aspect of life; for example, the metaphor 'plant a seed of doubt' is from the semantic field of gardening.

Using context (AO3)

You will be expected to show knowledge of relevant context. This could relate to Jacobean society or a modern audience's expectations; the important thing is to make sure it really is relevant and not just 'bolted on' to your argument for the sake of it.

15 Read these two extracts from student essays on the role of Iago. Annotate what you think are their good and bad points. Which do you think uses context more effectively? Write an 'examiner' comment beneath each one.

(a)   Iago is an ensign – a flag-holder, and in a sense he carries the flag

for a particular sort of crass male chauvinism, seeing sex in animal

terms as 'making the beast with two backs' and assuming that

Desdemona will tire of Othello 'when she is sated with his body'.

At the same time his suspicion that Othello has 'done [his] office'

with Emilia reflects the particular male horror of being cuckolded

CONTINUED ➤

that was typical of the era. A Jacobean audience might see him
as representing the motiveless villainy of a medieval mystery
play devil, but a modern one is more likely to see him as sexually
motivated, or even as a psychopath.

....

....

....

....

....

....

(b)   Shakespeare's audience would see Iago as being like a devil,
just doing evil for the sake of it. At the same time they might
sympathise with him because they were a lot more racist in those
days and this could be seen as a motive for Iago to resent Othello.
Elizabeth I even issued two edicts to get black people removed
from England, though there cannot have been that many. Even
Iago's harsh treatment of Emilia is not all that bad in the context
of the period, because it was normal for men to dominate women
and expect them to obey without question, as when Iago gets
Emilia to steal Desdemona's handkerchief.

....

....

....

....

....

CONTINUED ➡

Answers can be found at: www.hoddereducation.co.uk/workbookanswers

Exploring connections across texts (AO4)

Depending on your syllabus, you may be asked to compare *Othello* with other texts. The type of connection that will be relevant to any syllabus is founded in the genre of tragedy.

16 You should know at least one other Shakespeare play. Make notes on how it compares with *Othello* using the table below.

	OTHELLO	OTHER PLAY
What triggers the main action?		
How is there confusion and disorder during the central part of the play?		
How is the disorder resolved?		
How does love of any kind feature?		
What types of imagery dominate?		
How are settings used?		

17 *Othello* has been called a 'domestic tragedy', centring on a marriage, not on matters of state like *Macbeth*, *Hamlet* or *King Lear*. In your view does this make it less significant? Explain your ideas.

....

....

....

....

CONTINUED ➔

18 Read the following account of Shakespeare's comedy *Much Ado About Nothing*. Then write one or more paragraphs comparing it with *Othello*.

Don Pedro (a lord), Benedick and Count Claudio come back victorious from war. Claudio falls in love with a virtuous young woman, Hero. In a subplot, Benedick and Beatrice (Hero's cousin) enjoy playful rivalry but eventually fall in love.

Don Pedro has a cynical and melancholic illegitimate brother, Don John, who calls himself a 'plain-dealing villain'. Don John only gets satisfaction from creating 'mischief', and he resents Claudio's position in Don Pedro's affections. Don John and his follower Borachio trick Claudio into thinking Hero has been unfaithful by arranging for Claudio to see Hero's maid embracing Borachio at the window.

Claudio, believing the maid to be Hero, waits till their marriage day and shames her at the altar, jilting her and calling her a 'rotten orange'. She is so shocked by the shame and injustice that she faints and is assumed dead. Claudio eventually repents somewhat, and is persuaded to marry Hero's 'sister', who is really Hero.

....

....

....

....

....

....

....

....

....

....

....

....

....

....

....

....

CONTINUED ➡

....

....

....

Interpretations (AO5)

19 One way to develop your own interpretation of the play is to consider those of critics. Read John Bayley's assessment below, from his *Tragedy and Consciousness*.

Othello brings us face to face with the problem not elsewhere encountered in the tragedies, or indeed in Shakespeare's works in general: the distinction between tragic and comic. Normally the question doesn't arise. But it does here, because, to paraphrase Horace Walpole's *mot*, the play is tragic if we can feel a part of it, comic if we look at it from the outside. And the distinction, like all such distinctions where *Othello* is concerned, is very absolute and abrupt. Nothing could be more surprising, in a way, than to find a tension between comic and tragic treatment suddenly making itself felt.

And it was sensed early on. Writing at the end of the same century in which *Othello* was first produced Thomas Rymer called the play 'a bloody farce'. Noun and adjective brings the ideas of comedy and tragedy together in their most depreciatory sense, and no more accurately unsympathetic judgement on the play has ever been made. In our own time more genteel, but also more intellectualized versions of Rymer's disfavour have been voiced by T. S. Eliot and F. R. Leavis, who both consider and reject the personality that Othello presents to the outside world, pointing out that he is not so much deceived as a self-deceiver, a man presented by Shakespeare as constitutionally incapable of seeing the truth about himself.

Make notes on the main critical points in this extract.

....

....

....

....

....

....

....

....

....

....

CONTINUED ➡

....

....

....

....

....

....

....

TAKING IT FURTHER

20 Bearing in mind the points you noted for **Activity 19**, plan and write a 500-word essay exploring the view that '*Othello* has so much in common with comedy, that it does not have the status of a true tragedy.'

21 Read Act 3, scene 3, from Othello's 'Give me a living reason ...' (412) to the end of the scene. On a separate sheet, comment in detail on how Shakespeare presents Iago's persuasion of Othello.

You could consider:

- Iago's technique and how Othello responds to it
- the effect of imagery
- the dramatic impact on the audience.

22 Referring back to **Activity 6**, plan and write on a separate sheet a full response to this question:

'Explore the view that the female characters in *Othello* are only of secondary importance.'

23 Read this full response to the question first given in **Activity 6**.

(a) Annotate it, identifying the strengths highlighted and what Assessment Objectives they fulfil. (See the start of this chapter for a list of the AOs.)

Othello certainly reflects the <u>male social dominance of Jacobean England. Brabantio is outraged that Desdemona has eloped with someone he would never have chosen. He complains of his 'despised time' and 'bitterness' (Act 1, scene 1) because he will now suffer loss of face. This is his first concern, not Desdemona's happiness. Othello is a 'foul thief' who has stolen his property. When Desdemona is summoned (Act 1, scene 3), she dutifully acknowledges that she now owes obedience to Othello.</u>[1]

In addition, the play's male characters have more lines than its female ones, and it is called Othello's tragedy, not Desdemona's – which could be compared with <u>the dual focus of 'Romeo and Juliet'.</u>[2] The fact that

CONTINUED ➡

Answers can be found at: www.hoddereducation.co.uk/workbookanswers

female characters were played by boys is only a partial explanation.[3] Shakespeare seems to have been largely concerned with Othello's transformation. At first Othello has the calm self-confidence to tell his accusers, in Act 1, scene 2, 'Keep up your bright swords.' However, thanks to Iago, he gradually breaks down, his disjointed language showing his disintegration: 'Pish! Noses, ears and lips. Is't possible?' (Act 4, scene 1).

Desdemona goes through no similar transformation, merely moving from confident happiness to puzzled distress. This suggests that Shakespeare was less interested in her, although critic AJ Honigmann argues that it shows her greater constancy.[4]

The plot is at first driven by male concerns. Othello is sent to Cyprus to tackle the Turks by the all-male Venetian senate. Iago's scheming is provoked by hatred of Othello and his resentment of his rival Cassio, whom he sneeringly dismisses as 'a great arithmetician', ignorant of real war (Act 1, scene 1). He launches his campaign in the male setting of a drunken brawl between soldiers (Act 2, scene 3).[5]

The play's maleness is also seen in its maritime imagery, as in Othello's metaphorical 'sea-mark of my utmost sail' (Act 5, scene 2), and images of entrapment and imprisonment, as in Iago's reference to 'the net that shall enmesh them all' (Act 2, scene 3). Even the grossness of the sexual animal imagery, such as Iago's 'an old black ram/ Is tupping your white ewe!' (Act 1, scene 1), seems characteristically masculine, even to modern audiences.[6]

Although the women are marginalised, they are important dramatically. Othello's military world is contrasted with domesticity when Desdemona insists that she pleads for Cassio only for Othello's own good, as if asking him to wear gloves or eat nourishing food (Act 3, scene 3). When she asks when he will speak to Cassio, she

CONTINUED ➔

suggests mealtimes: 'tonight at supper', 'Tomorrow dinner'. <u>She is also vital to the plot as it is love that makes Othello vulnerable. Similarly, Cassio is vulnerable to Iago's scheming because of his Bianca. It is Emilia who enables Iago's use of the handkerchief as 'evidence', yet it is also Emilia who bravely exposes his treachery.</u>[7]

Male attitudes to women are crucial in the play. Othello at first adores Desdemona as his 'soul's joy'. Cassio almost worships her as a goddess whose beauty overcomes the 'mortal natures' of winds and seas (Act 2, scene 1). Iago has no respect for women or for Emilia. When she says she has something for him, <u>he dismisses it out of hand as 'a common thing'. His contempt means that it never occurs to him that she will expose him.</u>[8]

Though given fewer lines, the female characters are strong in their own ways. Desdemona defies her father to marry a Moor, and insists on going to Cyprus with him. Some critics say that she is passive, dutifully allowing her own murder, but she is still in shock at being accused. Bianca breaks the mould of the 'strumpet' by being devoted to Cassio – she counts the hours since she saw him last (Act 3, scene 4), but also stands up to him. <u>Emilia is passionately committed to justice in her wish that villains should be whipped round the world (Act 4, scene 2), and in her 'feminist' speech asserting women's needs and desires (Act 4, scene 3). She also fiercely defends Desdemona to Othello and dies accusing Iago.</u>[9]

Finally, the play's most powerful symbol – the handkerchief – is feminine. It was made by a prophetess, given by an Egyptian woman to Othello's mother, and it now belongs to Desdemona. Since it is said to have magical power, and is the means by which Iago convinces Othello of Desdemona's guilt, it assumes huge dramatic significance.

CONTINUED